MW01715867

Chris

Be a leader!

Make a difference!

Paul B. Thornton

THE ANSWERS ARE ON THE OFFICE WALL

THE ANSWERS ARE ON THE OFFICE WALL

PAUL B. THORNTON

MONOCHROME Press

Subsidiary of Gray Media, Inc.
Exeter, New Hampshire

ISBN: 1-882407-08-3

Library of Congress Catalog Card Number: 94-76837

Text and jacket design by Christine Swirnoff

Illustration by Robert J. Lamontagne

Manufactured in the United States of America by Maple-Vail Book Manufacturing Group

10 9 8 7 6 5 4 3 2 1

Dedicated to three special people—

Mary Jean,

Kate,

and Andrew.

Acknowledgments

I would like to thank the following friends and business associates for reading the manuscript and providing valuable suggestions, feedback, and encouragement: Dan Kelly, Dave Gonyea, Steve Ludemann, Dennis Ericson, Jim Bagnall, Joanne Hastings, Rick Narowski, Andrea Yurcak, Bob Fraleigh, Jennifer Powell, Eric Schneider, John Cardinal, Art Wanderlingh, John Nicoletta, Phil Beaudoin, Rick Kretschmar, Al Wolf, Ralf Schluter, Joanne Cleary, Jabe Luttrell, Ingrid Delgado, Debbie Cosmar, John Lashnits, Roy Butler, John Mayo, and Jim Ligotti.

Special thanks to my wife, Mary Jean, who was always willing to discuss the manuscript and provide her ideas and insights about the changes going on in the business world. In addition, I'd like to thank my daughter Kate for reading my material and giving me feedback from a 17-year-old's point of view.

Hal Taylor, Ben Bishop, Joel Esten, Steve Bennett, and John Frasca deserve special thanks for providing me with several business examples that directly related to several office wall quotes. Steve Worthington and Alden Davis were also a tremendous help in sending me a number of office wall quotes they came across in doing their jobs.

Robert J. Lamontagne also deserves a special thanks for designing and creating a great illustration that shows how people resist change.

Thanks also go to my editor and publisher, Dana Scannell, for being open to my ideas and being committed to producing a quality book. In addition, Marcy Gage, Chris Gray, and Allison Gray all deserve credit for their roles in making this book a reality.

And finally I'd like to thank my mother, Elizabeth Thornton. She was the first person to review the manuscript and she said, "It's good, but keep working at it and you'll make it great."

Introduction

People want to know what it takes to succeed in today's competitive, dynamic, and challenging business world. What are the new rules of the game? How do you stand out from the crowd? How do you get ahead and achieve career goals?

I believe the answers to these and similar questions are right there in front of you on the office wall. Successful people often write down and post the key ideas and attitudes required for success. Wall postings such as "Take care of the customer or someone else will," "Be realistic—demand the impossible," and "When you're through learning, you're through" are thoughtful reminders of what it takes to compete in today's business world. Many of these wall postings provide great advice on a range of topics, including customer satisfaction, communication, change, continuous improvement, productivity, quality, teamwork, leadership, and attitudes.

What follows is a collection of my favorite wall postings and, accompanying all of them, a brief discussion of the change or changes you must make to succeed in your business and career.

As you read this book, keep this office wall quote in mind:

"Change Produces Temporary Pain, Not Changing Produces Permanent Pain."

STAY IN COMFORT ZONE!
DON'T OVERDO IT
NO SWEAT
EASY DOES IT
IF IT AINT BROKE DON'T FIX IT
DO IT SOON
ENOUGH IS ENOUGH!
THAT'S GOOD ENOUGH
IN

HARRY, THE CULTURE CHANGE DOESN'T SEEM TO BE TAKING HOLD HERE
OUT

THE ANSWERS ARE ON THE OFFICE WALL

‘Take Care of the Customer or Someone Else Will’

Change from being "boss focused" to "customer focused." Bosses are important, but customers are the key. They pay your salary. One guy I know who's president of a big, successful aerospace company told me job security is not something the company president gives you—it's something that customers provide. When customers see how you care about your product, how you care about servicing them, and how you act like an owner—they continue to place orders, and that's what gives you job security.

The traditional focus has been vertical—please the boss. But if everyone is looking up to please the boss, who's looking horizontally where the customer is? Progressive companies believe that salespeople should pay more attention to their customers' needs than to their bosses' needs.

How well do you know your customers? Here are some questions you need to answer on an ongoing basis:

- What are my customers' problems and needs?
- How do my customers want to do business with me?
- What are their expectations of me?
- What type of product or service would make customers say "Wow!" or "Gee whiz, look at this"?

If you are not continually focused on your customers and getting them to say "Wow!" once in a while, then someone else will. Here's a good suggestion from Ron Willingham, author of *Hey, I'm the Customer*: Write down a set of "exit statements." That is, when customers leave or exit your store or work area, how do you want them to describe the product or service they received? How do you want them to describe the care and service you provided? If customers exit your area happy and satisfied, repeat business is guaranteed.

‘Excellence Means Your Customer Is Satisfied’

"Excellence Means Your Customer Is Satisfied"

Change your definition of customer satisfaction!

Heed the observation of Professor Ron Zemke: "Left to our own devices, we pay more and more attention to things of less and less importance to the customer." Not exactly a good strategy to grow your business or advance your career.

Are your customers satisfied? Why not ask them? Listen carefully to what they say. Many times a customer will say service was fine . . . but; or the quality is good . . . but. Don't stop listening after hearing the good stuff. When the customer says fine . . . but—that's the signal to listen aggressively and ask probing questions.

Three of my pet peeves are the following:

1. My health club uses the "Tell us how we can do better" cards. Three weeks in a row I filled out a card and said, "Fix the treadmill." After three weeks the treadmill still wasn't working.
2. Frequently when I get in line at a fast-food restaurant, I find that my line moves the slowest, compared with the other three or four lines.
3. When I buy a toy or product that requires assembly, I often find that the instruction booklet is confusing and difficult to read.

Why can't companies fix these problems? Find out what's important to your customer and then take the appropriate steps to have happy and satisfied customers.

Remember, how you or your company defines "customer satisfaction" is irrelevant! Customer satisfaction is defined by the customer and the customer alone.

‘Information Gains Power as It’s Shared’

"Information Gains Power as It's Shared"

Change your attitude from hoarding information to sharing information. Phone, fax, E-mail, write, meet, video—whatever it takes, but make sure to communicate!

Journalist Alan Webber said that in the old days if the boss caught you talking on the phone or hanging around the water cooler, he or she would have said, "Stop talking and get to work!" However, in today's dynamic, fast-paced information society, if you're not talking with customers, colleagues, or suppliers, the boss is likely to say, "Start talking and get to work!"

Knowledge—or intellectual capital, as it is now called—is useless unless it is continually received and spread through the organization. New ideas, new information, and lessons learned must be shared for the benefit of all.

Whom do you talk with? How broad is your communication network? With whom do you share your knowledge, ideas, and insights?

Your information network must include a broad range of customers, suppliers, competitors, and people at all levels of your organization, as well as successful people outside your industry. Here are two suggestions:

1. Select and send clippings broadly to your associates, customers, and suppliers with a note saying, "In case you missed this . . ." Chances are they will return the favor and keep you up-to-date.
2. When you read an interesting business article, call the author to further discuss the topic.

Follow these suggestions and watch your information network grow.

‘A Desk Is a Dangerous Place from Which to View the World’

"A Desk Is a Dangerous Place from Which to View the World"

Every day, spend some time away from your desk.

Honda of America stresses that management and support personnel must go to a trouble spot in the plant, see the problem, touch the part, talk with operators, and gain experience in the job process before trying to help solve the problem.

Go and look for yourself. Information often gets exaggerated, filtered, and misinterpreted as it passes from one individual to another. That's why it's often best to see and hear for yourself. Every day I try to spend 20 to 30 minutes walking through office and factory areas. I not only find out what people are thinking but I also get a view of people's work load, where production bottlenecks are occurring, and a sense of people's energy level and morale.

Another reason to get out of the office is to observe customers. Watch them use your product. Do they make any changes or adjustments to your product? What would make their job easier? Customers can't always articulate their needs, that's why observing them directly can provide valuable information.

My teenage daughter, Kate, returned home with a new pair of jeans. After showing me her purchase, she immediately started cutting holes in the knee area. As I watched I could feel my blood pressure rising. I said, "Kate, what are you doing?" She responded, "It's the in thing. I'm making these jeans look better." Apparently, the jeans manufacturer was also observing its customers. About a week later, jeans with precut holes in the knees were selling at retail stores.

Remember, there is no substitute for firsthand knowledge.

‘Less Data, More Meaning’

Change from giving "data dumps" to explaining the significance or meaning of the data.

Today, we are flooded with studies, reports, and computer runs that provide data about every conceivable aspect of business. The amount of data is overwhelming. What's often lacking is interpretation of the data—What does it mean? Employees are asking, "How does this data affect me?" "What's the impact on our team or business?" Your effectiveness is greatly enhanced when you provide an explanation of the data in such a way that people know what it means to them.

My experience is that people can deal with reality and the meaning of things much better than we often give them credit for. Therefore, avoid trying to put a positive gloss on the message. Develop the confidence and courage to be clear and precise. Jack Welch, the chief executive officer of General Electric, said that people fear being simple because they think they will be viewed as simple-minded. But in reality it's just the opposite. Intelligent, tough-minded people are the most simple, clear, and precise.

How can you simplify your message? One technique I use in preparing to make presentations is to ask this question: "What's the least number of words I can use to make the point or explain the chart?" This question helps me boil down the information to a simple and succinct message.

If you are having trouble being simple and clear, take the advice of this office wall quote: "If you can't explain it in two sentences, you shouldn't be doing the explaining." Find the person who will—keep it simple—and let him or her do the explaining.

‘Listen to the Pain’

Change from being "defensive" to being "open and receptive."

Pain is another term for bad news. Complaints from customers and negative feedback from your boss or associates may be the most useful news you receive. If you react defensively to bad news and don't listen, there's no opportunity to improve. On the other hand, if you listen calmly and with an open mind, you are taking the first step toward improving the situation. Take the time to listen to complaints and problems. Make it a priority. Ed McCracken, CEO of Silicon Graphics, has asserted that we can go out of business if we focus on market research about traditional customers. He urges us instead to listen to dissatisfied customers and then demand the appropriate changes in product or services.

Dr. Dennis Waitley, psychologist and author of *The Psychology of Winning*, states that pain is simply a signal for change. It tells me that I need to either change the way I do things or change the way I look at things. After I receive negative feedback, the first thing I do is take a "time-out." During the time-out I remind myself not to be defensive; instead, I take the attitude "What can I learn from this?" I try to analyze the feedback from three levels:

1. What's the overall message?
2. What are the important details of the message?
3. What should I do differently next time?

The more I pinpoint specific changes to be made, the more likely I am to make them.

Also remember, nobody wants to be the one to deliver bad news because that triggers the "kill the messenger" syndrome. If you're in charge, encourage the flow of bad news. If you don't, the problem only gets worse.

‘Behind
Every Open Door
Needs to Be
an Open Mind’

Change your attitude from the typical, “I’m open-minded but I know what works” to “I’m open. What worked or was successful in the past may not produce success in the future.”

I used to know a manager who passionately claimed he had an “open-door policy.” In a literal sense his door *was* open and he would talk with you, but he was the most close-minded person I know. His usual comment was, “Why change a good thing?” Some “good things” do need to change if you want to be successful in the future.

If you take credit for having an open-door policy, make sure your mind is also open. How can you make sure you keep an open mind? Try these:

- Realize that if you are receptive in all your contacts, you may discover a better idea or solution. Breakthrough ideas come from all corners of the organization.
- Don’t assume or prejudge. Use focus words like “open up” or “don’t judge” as reminders to keep an open mind.
- Seek to understand the speaker’s reality. What experiences has the person had that have led to his or her belief or viewpoint?

Whether you agree with a person or not, listen and keep an open mind. If the idea has merit, why not try it for a week or a month? In most cases, if the new idea doesn’t work, you can always revert to the original practice.

And remember, personal growth doesn’t take place unless you allow access to new thoughts, feelings, and ideas. Access is gained only by being “open.” Here’s another office wall quote that makes the point rather well—“You’re not listening when you hear only what you want to hear.”

“There Was an Important Job to Be Done and Everybody Was Asked to Do It. Everybody Was Sure Somebody Would Do It. Anybody Could Have Done It. But Nobody Did.”

"There Was an Important Job to Be Done and Everybody Was Asked to Do It. Everybody Was Sure Somebody Would Do It. Anybody Could Have Done It. But Nobody Did."

Change from using "vague, general words" to using "clear and specific" words.

Communication breakdowns occur every day. Only "effective" communications will improve your overall results. Words like: everybody, somebody, and anybody lead to confusion and misunderstandings.

When I'm involved in a communication breakdown, I try to trace back and pinpoint why it happened. Very often the villain is a vague or imprecise word that was interpreted other than intended. For example, a "significant improvement" might be interpreted as a 10% improvement or a 50% improvement. The phrase, "as soon as possible"—does that mean do it in the next two minutes, two hours, or two days? Using more specific language helps reduce confusion.

You also need to be very clear and specific when assigning tasks or responsibilities. Making people vaguely responsible or accountable doesn't work. For best results, define and get agreement on who is responsible for what actions, when the task is to be completed, and how results will be measured. Sometimes it's wise to define responsibilities in writing as well as discuss them verbally. My wife, Mary Jean, says that when you make responsibility and ownership crystal clear, communication gets real simple.

If things are not completed as expected, ask yourself, "What didn't I do to ensure success?" Don't start by blaming others. A teacher once told me that when you point your finger, you still have three fingers pointing back at yourself!

‘Don’t Assume’

Change from making assumptions to questioning assumptions.

A friend of mine visits the former Soviet Union several times each year. On a recent business trip he visited a local art gallery, where he found a painting he wanted to buy. He asked the artist the cost of the painting. The artist said, "Sixty dollars, but sorry, already sold." Unable to find another painting he liked, he asked the artist if he would paint him the picture he liked. The artist said that he would and that it would be delivered to his hotel on his next trip. On his next trip the painting was delivered as promised—with a bill for $12,000. My friend assumed the painting would cost $60. The Russian artist assumed that all Americans are naive and wealthy.

Making assumptions can be costly and confusing. Have you ever found yourself saying:

"I thought you meant . . ."

"I assumed you knew how to do it."

"I assumed there was no hurry."

"I assumed you wanted it done this way."

Your failure to communicate effectively may lead you and others down the wrong path. Don't assume you understood. Probe. Ask questions. Define terms. Make sure you and the other person are on the same wavelength. During the Sixties when I was in college, one of the T-shirt slogans read, "Question authority." Today's version could be "Question assumptions."

“I Know You Believe
You Understand
What I Said,
but
I’m Not Sure You Realize
That What You Heard
Is Not What I Meant”

"I Know You Believe You Understand What I Said, but I'm Not Sure You Realize That What You Heard Is Not What I Meant"

Don't believe that what people say is always what they mean!

When my 17-year-old daughter, Kate, says "That's great," it can mean (1) "Great news," (2) "Not that again," or (3) "You've ruined my life." Further, "my life" usually refers to the next dance, party, or social engagement.

Let's face it, communication is a difficult process whether you're the sender or receiver. When you throw a baseball or football to someone you can watch and see if it's caught. When ideas are thrown back and forth, it's often difficult to know what's understood and not understood. Here are some suggestions to improve communications:

- Always make eye contact with the speaker. Eye contact is a good reminder to pay attention and listen.
- Be aware of body language, tone of voice, and how the message is delivered. This information often gives you clues to the "real" message.
- Ask questions, and probe for the feelings that underlie the statements.
- When your attention wanders, use focus words like "Tune in," "Concentrate," or "Stop" as reminders to listen.
- Test the transfer. Feed back to the speaker your understanding of his or her message.

And remember, sometimes what people say is actually the opposite of what they think or feel!

‘Take Time to Think.
In Order to
Do Things
Differently,
You Must
See Things
Differently.’

"Take Time to Think. In Order to Do Things Differently, You Must See Things Differently."

Change from simply reacting to urgent things to taking time to think about important things.

Many days, it feels as if you arrive at work, jump on the business treadmill, and go, go, go. There's no time to think. The day is spent reacting to urgent things like ringing phones, people at your desk, and meetings. But remember, you can be busy, very busy, without being effective.

Periodically, you need to stop the treadmill, get off, and quietly think about what's going on. How can you be more effective? Try answering these questions:

- Does your customer value all aspects of the products and services you provide? Could some be eliminated?
- How much time do you spend putting out fires versus solving root-cause problems?
- How much time do you spend on short-term planning versus long-term planning?
- Could parts of your job be eliminated or automated?
- Could some tasks be delegated to someone else?
- How does your operation look from the customer's point of view? Your supplier's point of view? Your co-workers' point of view?

As they say, it's hard to see the forest when your day is spent cutting down trees. It's hard to change if you don't stop, step back, and reflect on your performance and effectiveness.

‘Good Enough Isn’t Good Enough. Better Is What Counts!’

Change your attitude from "I improved the results once and I'm done" to "I've improved the results once and I'll do it again, and again, and again." Continuous improvement must be your way of life because your competition is improving daily.

About 10 years ago I reported to a feisty, white-haired manager whose favorite expression was "If it ain't broke, don't fix it." Every time I suggested a new human resources program, he'd say, "Paul, if it ain't broke, don't fix it." In today's global marketplace, it's a different ball game.

Bruce Gissing, an executive vice president at Boeing Aircraft Company, made the point well when he said that since it ain't perfect, try to improve it, make it more reliable and less costly to produce. Another office wall quote I observed at a high-tech company states, "Best is the enemy of better." Just when we convince ourselves we have the *best* product, the *best* technology, the *best* training program, someone shows up with something better. Don't think "best," because that makes you complacent. Think "better." How can I make it or do it better?

I believe most people have gotten the "improvement message" and have taken steps to improve their process once or twice. The real task though is getting up for the "change and improve" challenge again and again. Continuous improvement is a lifelong endeavor.

Remember, the attitude "That's good enough" will guarantee loss in the marketplace and perhaps loss of your job!

‘If You
Always Do
What You
Always Did,
You Will
Always Get
What You
Always Got’

"If You Always Do What You Always Did, You Will Always Get What You Always Got"

Change your behavior!

I have several relatives who frequently talk about losing weight, eating a more balanced diet, and exercising on a regular basis. The only problem is they never take the next step and change their behavior or, if they do, it lasts for only a few days or weeks.

A similar office wall quote states, "Insanity is hoping for different results while continuing to do the same thing." Just "hoping" isn't enough. Change is needed. Change is often difficult, uncomfortable, and stressful. That's why it's avoided. But change is needed to produce different results.

The ability to change the way you operate to match the changing needs of customers is a prerequisite for survival in the marketplace. Once you have identified the change, you may try these techniques:

- Keep a focus on the business reasons that the change is needed.
- Establish a deadline to begin the new behavior.
- Announce publicly the change(s) you are making and why.
- Reward yourself after you have changed behavior for a two-week period.

Company president and author Harvey Mackay is among those who have urged us to adapt to change. He points to the recurring life cycle of birth, growth, and death, and reminds us that the same repeated pattern exists in the marketplace. Businesspeople who want to survive, he says, learn to identify patterns and transform them into opportunities.

‘Destroy the Dominant Paradigm’

Change the paradigm. Yesterday's paradigm may not fit today's reality.

A paradigm is an attitude, belief, or viewpoint about how things should look and function. For example, we have a distinct view of what a hockey stick or bicycle seat should look like. We also have rules or paradigms about designing products, running meetings, treating customers, and developing employees.

Challenge these paradigms! Question their logic, their applicability, their usefulness! Breakthrough ideas often result when you seriously question—"Why do we do it that way?" Sam Walton, the founder of Walmart, said that he always prided himself on breaking everybody else's rules and favored the mavericks who challenged his rules.

Under the old paradigm, the good employee was someone who "went along to get along." If you didn't like what the boss wanted to do, you sat on your hands. Now you are encouraged to challenge the status quo and speak up about better ways to operate. Survival means challenging your own past successes. Don't overly identify with, lock on to, or feel secured to any particular product, process, or way of doing business. If you do, you will miss opportunities for new products and better ways of working.

How do you change a paradigm? I like to take a current belief or viewpoint and list all the assumptions and ideas that support it. Next, I randomly change assumptions and see what new ideas emerge. Every once in a while I discover a breakthrough idea that produces a totally different and better method of operation.

Remember, a new paradigm frees you from the past and allows you to see new opportunities, new relationships, and new ways of working.

‘Those Who Say It Can’t Be Done Should Get Out of the Way of Those Who Are Already Doing It’

"Those Who Say It Can't Be Done Should Get Out of the Way of Those Who Are Already Doing It"

Change your attitude and change what's possible.

Between 1980 and 1984, I was the varsity hockey coach at a small New England college. During my second year, I learned a lot about "attitudes." In one game, we played the University of Massachusetts. After the first period, U-Mass was ahead 5-1. In the locker room between periods, players' body language and comments indicated negative attitudes—"We're done. Chalk this one up in the lost column." I fed back to the group what I was seeing and hearing. I wanted them to be crystal clear in realizing the attitude they were expressing. Once they realized how negative they were, they started to change. As attitudes changed, play on the ice improved. In the second period we scored two quick goals and now everyone was a believer. We went on to win the game 10-8. Whenever I hear people say, "It can't be done," I think back to this game.

Your attitude sets the boundaries of what you achieve. In my house family members expressing negative attitudes are confronted and asked to do an "attitude check." This is a reminder to stop and listen to what you're saying. Changing our attitude is often the first step toward looking at the problem differently. Pat Riley, coach of the New York Knicks basketball team, says that people who keep breaking records are those who keep doing inner research. They develop attitudes and different themes about what it takes to go above and beyond.

If the new approach doesn't exist, why don't you be the first to say, "I'm going to discover a better way"? Figure out how you can be the one who comes up with the next great idea.

‘Have You Challenged a Sacred Cow Lately? Is There Value to Justify Its Existence? If Not, Make Hamburg’

"Have You Challenged a Sacred Cow Lately? Is There Value to Justify Its Existence? If Not, Make Hamburg"

Change your attitude that "sacred cows" are not sacred.

Sacred cows are all those beliefs, behaviors, policies, and practices that people think are untouchable. They can't be questioned. But to succeed today, you must not consider anything "sacred." Question every policy and procedure. Dispute the attitude "That's the way we have always done it."

Management consultant Price Pritchett said that instead of blindly accepting old beliefs and attitudes, throw them against the rocks of reality and see if they shatter. If you're willing to smash some glass, you may discover some new ideas about running your business and satisfying your customers. Be prepared to abandon some of your own cherished attitudes, beliefs, and behaviors. Today's rapidly changing business world requires you to keep learning and experimenting.

Harry Quadrucci, CEO of Quad/Graphics, has challenged many business practices. His advice: Eliminate budgets, junk your time clock, and sell off the purchasing department. How about this—encourage meditating as a way to stimulate the creative process.

One of the "sacred cows" I'm attacking deals with performance appraisals. Since employees own, or are responsible for, their own performance, why not also make them responsible for soliciting and evaluating feedback on their performance. Require employees to periodically obtain feedback from a variety of sources, including customers, supervisor, team members, peers, etc. This type of performance feedback is more meaningful.

What "sacred cows" are you attacking?

‘Why?’

Ask "Why" and "What if" at least a dozen times every day!

Bruce Gissing, executive vice president at Boeing Aircraft Company, said that world-class managers are genuinely curious. One of their favorite questions is "Why?" Why is this activity necessary? Why is that procedure followed? Why do we need that rule? An executive at Kodak says, "If someone says it takes six months to do something, I say, 'Why can't we do it in a month?' "

Imagine the power of constantly, incessantly questioning every report, rule, policy, system, process, and procedure with that simple question—Why are we doing this?

Recently I've begun to think my 14-year-old son, Andrew, is on his way to becoming a world-class manager. Every time I ask him or tell him to do something, he asks "Why?" "Why do I have to clean my room? Why do I have to do my homework?" Actually, I don't think that's exactly what Bruce Gissing had in mind.

Another good question to ask is "What if?" The inventor of Nike shoes asked, "What happens if I pour rubber into my waffle iron?" That simple what-if question revolutionized the athletic shoe industry. What-if questions can plant seeds for people to consider a wide range of new ideas and possibilities. For example:

- What if we change the material or the shape?
- What if we invite customers to our staff meetings?
- What if we eliminate that job?

Remember, don't lose your sense of curiosity. Albert Einstein once said that the important thing is to keep questioning. And always be thinking of "new" questions to ask.

'This Is a Revolution, Not an Evolution'

Change from "slow and steady" to "fast and furious."

Evolution means slow, gradual change. Revolution, on the other hand, means rapid and profound change. Today, customer expectations, global competition, and new technologies are radically altering how work is done.

Ralph S. Larsen, chairman and chief executive officer, Johnson & Johnson, said that his senior management team realized it wasn't enough to play by the old rules—the game itself had to be changed.

Many companies are currently undergoing "reengineering," which involves fundamental rethinking and radical redesign of business processes. These are achieving dramatic improvements in cost, quality, and speed. This type of major change can be upsetting, frustrating, and anxiety-provoking. Most people want to stay in their comfort zone. What can you do? Try these:

- Seek to understand the reasons changes are needed.
- Be open and receptive to change. The new work method may be more appealing than the old one.
- Don't focus on everything you're giving up—list the positive aspects of the new situation.

Step back and try to be an outside objective observer to your own behavior. How many times have you watched your favorite sports team and said (usually about halfway through the game), "Those idiots! Why don't they just change what they are doing!" Be willing to consider and try new and different ways of working. Be willing to take risks and try new approaches.

‘When You’re Through Learning, You’re Through’

Change from "no more homework" to "lifelong learning!"

Top managers at Stew Leonard's Dairy in Norwalk, Connecticut, regularly take groups of employees on "One Idea Club" field trips. They travel to other supermarkets, where each employee is expected to find one idea he or she will try to use back on the job. Are you looking for new and more effective ways of doing your job?

I spend at least two hours per night doing homework—reading and studying various business topics. My 14-year-old son, Andrew, recently said to me, "I thought you only had homework in school!" Not so. Lifelong learning and, yes, homework are required to compete in today's business Olympics.

Never stop educating yourself through:

- Workshops and seminars
- Continuing education classes
- Company in-house training programs
- Asking questions
- Reading books, magazines, and newspapers
- Observing how successful people and companies operate

Those who constantly learn and retool themselves have a much better chance of staying employed. "What you don't know won't hurt you" doesn't work these days. Work hardest on the areas you are least familiar with. It's human nature to work in our "comfort zone," but we grow when we study and learn new skills and techniques.

‘Childlike Qualities We Should All Keep— Curiosity, Playfulness, Open-mindedness, Willingness to Experiment, Living in the Present, Forgiveness, Flexibility, and Honesty’

"Childlike Qualities We Should All Keep—Curiosity, Playfulness, Open-mindedness, Willingness to Experiment, Living in the Present, Forgiveness, Flexibility, and Honesty"

Change from acting like an adult to acting like a child.

The next time you are at the playground, observe the young children. They thrive on change. Children move from one activity to another with curiosity and a willingness to learn and experiment. They are never rigid in their approach; rather, they are flexible, always willing to try something new.

They don't worry about the past or the future. Kids live in and enjoy the present moment. They don't overanalyze situations, gathering all the facts, but rather follow their instincts and intuition. They do what "feels" right.

The movie "Big," which is one of my favorites, shows the advantages of maintaining childlike qualities. In the movie, Tom Hanks plays a child who has been magically transformed into an adult's body. He works in the marketing department of a toy company. In scene after scene, his attributes are shown to be in sharp contrast to those of the real adults who work at this company.

He's honest —	They play office politics
He's spontaneous —	They overengineer
He's intuitive —	They deal only with facts and figures
He's willing to experiment —	They're locked into "only one way to do it."

As adults, we can learn a great deal about dealing with change by watching and observing children.

‘Be Indignant About Mediocrity’

Change from average to outstanding!

Many people like being on top. Unfortunately, it's the top of the bell curve—the average section. Don't settle for average. The business world has some people who are very content with average performance and average results. These people use lackluster language, deliver blah presentations, and develop ho-hum solutions to problems. Recently I attended a presentation by one of these bland types. He used 70 overhead slides for a one-hour presentation. His presentation lacked any hint of passion or excitement.

Get excited about your job and career. Heed the advice of this company president who's struggling in a very competitive industry. Speaking to his employees, he had this to say: "We need you here, fully, every day. We need your total commitment and involvement. We need your enthusiasm. When you walk in, leave your blahs in the car."

Another office wall quote has a simple but powerful message—"Raise your standards. Past good performance won't make it in the future." The self-fulfilling prophecy is well documented. What you expect is what you get. When you expect more of yourself, you typically achieve more.

Don't settle for what's comfortable and easy. Challenge the boundaries you set for yourself. Don't lose your zest for adventure, for taking a risk, for doing something that no one has done before. The greatest waste of our natural resources is the number of people who never try to achieve their potential. Arthur C. Clarke said that the only way of discovering the limits of the possible is to venture a little way past them into the impossible.

Remember, in today's fast-paced, brutally competitive business environment, average or mediocre performers don't stay around very long.

‘Innovate or Evaporate’

"Innovate or Evaporate"

Change from doing the "usual" to experimenting with new and better ways of working.

Competitive pressure requires you to make the product faster, cheaper, and better. Constant innovation is needed. Companies that have the motto "Business as usual" are filing for Chapter 11 bankruptcy. Michael Sinyard of Specialized Inc., inventor of the mountain bike, teaches his employees a slogan: "Innovate or die!"

Fresh, creative ideas have become the most precious raw material in the world. Spend time every week trying to create new products and more efficient ways of working. Try these:

- Look at things backward.
- Rearrange the order.
- Combine unrelated items.
- Imagine yourself inside the problem looking out.
- Ask a 12-year-old child how he or she would solve the problem.
- Imagine your product being used in a totally different context.
- Attend trade shows.
- Seek input from innovative customers and suppliers.

Don't be afraid of making mistakes. Innovation almost always grows out of trial-and-error learning. The more attempts you make, the quicker you gain insight and the faster you discover breakthrough ideas. Management consultant Price Pritchett says that on the surface it sounds irresponsible, but to flourish today you actually need to make more mistakes. Fail quickly, and then recover and try something else.

Remember: Your competition is working hard to improve their processes and products. Today it's the survival of the fittest.

‘Be Realistic— Demand the Impossible’

Change from expecting "a lot" to demanding "the impossible" of yourself and others.

Step-change improvements are happening every day. Many companies are achieving significant increases in productivity, radical reductions in cost and cycle time, and impressive improvements in quality. Being realistic means you must achieve the same types of step-change improvements just to stay in the game. T. J. Rodgers, founder and CEO of Cypress Semiconductor, follows this advice and has this sign posted in his office.

Demand the impossible! We make an assumption that people will give up if presented with an impossible goal. Remember the old advice that goals should be "challenging but attainable." No one ever said "Impossible!" But what happens when you set impossible targets? People must think of totally new and different ways to get the job done. The old paradigm, the old way of working, won't cut it. Breakthrough ideas often come when you are forced to reinvent your job.

Therefore, don't request a 5 percent improvement in results, demand a 100 percent improvement. A friend of mine who is an organizational change consultant has this sign on his office wall: "A step-function change in results requires a step-function change in behavior, which requires a step-function change in thinking."

Donald Trump says that if you are going to be thinking anyway, you may as well think big. Thinking small, staying in your comfort zone will ultimately put you behind your competition.

‘Vital Few Versus Trivial Many’

Change from working on what's "quick and easy" to working on what's "significant and impactful."

I'm sitting in my office staring at a 5-inch pile of paperwork on my desk. One item involves rewriting a supervisor's policy guide. An up-to-date guide will significantly reduce my workload because supervisors will know the policies without having to call me. I'm tempted to reach for the simpler, easy-to-do paperwork, but then I remember the 80/20 rule.

The 80/20 rule was revealed when Vilfredo Pareto, an Italian economist and sociologist, discovered that 80 percent of Italy's wealth was in the hands of 20 percent of the population.

This rule applies to most activities in the business world. For example, 20 percent of what is in your in-basket is important and 80 percent is not.

Successful people share one common characteristic above all others: They know how to keep focused on their top priorities. Actually it's easy to get distracted. In a typical day most people perform dozens of different activities and get interrupted 10 times or more. In this environment you can be drawn into working on tasks that are low in priority but high on popularity.

Maintaining focus requires concentration and written reminders . . . concentration is to give your full, undivided attention to the present moment. If your attention begins to wander, using signal words like "focus" or "concentrate" can help jolt you back into the present moment.

Written reminders also help keep you on course. Many successful people write down their top four to six priorities for the year, month, week, and day. They post them in their work area and read them once a day. Also in preparing for meetings or presentations it's helpful to write down your top priorities.

Focus on the vital few; everything else will take care of itself.

‘After All Is Said and Done— More Is Said Than Done’

If you say it, do it.

I attend lots of meetings where participants go on at length about how their ideas will solve problems x, y, and z. Or how their ideas will increase sales, reduce costs, and improve quality. You can have the best ideas in the world, but customers and upper management value and recognize the person who turns ideas into action. No successful person has been described as being long on philosophy and short on implementation.

Don't be all talk, no action. If you make a commitment, live up to it. Remember how you felt when the repairman said that he would be at your house at 9 a.m., but didn't show up until 4 p.m.! Nothing impresses a customer more than a person who keeps promises.

Whenever I need new tires for my car, I go to a store in Springfield, Massachusetts. There are lots of tire stores, but I keep returning to this one because the owner/manager is a real professional. He is dependable and reliable and always delivers on his promises. He has this sign hanging on his office wall: "A professional is someone who can do his best work even when he doesn't feel like it."

One additional point—the customer doesn't want surprises. I know I don't. The Mercury engine for my boat was supposed to be repaired and ready for pickup at noontime. I arrived at ll:45 a.m. and was told, "We ran into some problems; it's going to take two to three more hours." If there is a problem, let the customer know immediately and then take steps to fix it. Experts and business owners agree: Ignoring a problem, passing it off to someone else, and allowing a lot of time to pass before dealing with it are all guaranteed ways of losing customers.

'Don't Just Do Something, Stand There'

There are times when you need to "plan" first and "do it" later.

When I was growing up, my father frequently said, "Don't just stand there, do something." I'm not sure that what I ended up doing usually added value to the project. Sometimes I just tried to look busy and give the impression that I was helping.

You've heard the Nike advertisement "Just do it." That's great if you know what "it" is. Many times when people just jump in and start to do something, their efforts are in vain. They're fighting the wrong fire or solving the wrong problem.

Sometimes it's best to stand there and think. What's the goal or objective? Who owns the problem? What does the customer expect? What would happen if nothing was done? What information and people are needed to solve this problem?

Josh Weston, chairman and CEO of Automatic Data Processing (ADP), says that you need to set aside time to think. "At ADP, 39 plus 1 adds up to more than 40 plus zero. A 39-plus-one employee takes at least one hour of those 40 hours to think about what he's doing and why he's doing it. That's why the other 39 hours are far more productive," states Weston.

Plan before you act! However, realize that some problems and opportunities won't wait for you to come up with the perfect plan. Rapid change requires rapid responses. So don't always strive for the "perfect plan." Sometimes you have to "get ready" and "get going" at the same time.

“A Prescription Without a Diagnosis Is Malpractice”

Change from "giving answers" to "asking questions."

Beware of people who have a solution before they understand the problem. Suppose you have been having trouble with your eyes and you go to an optometrist for help. You walk into his office and without any examination he hands you a pair of glasses and says, "Try these, I think your problem is solved." Sounds silly, but in business there is a tendency by some to start designing systems, forms, and procedures without understanding the real problem.

An engineering manager states, "I used to quiz job applicants for software engineering positions by giving them a list of 10 common errors in software development. I asked them which error was most important to avoid. Anyone who picked No. 4, 'I didn't know the real problem to be solved,' was hired. Few did; however, those who did were terrific."

Often, the hardest part of problem-solving is figuring out what the real problem is. The most dangerous assumption you can make is that the problem is correctly stated. You need to dissect the facts, feelings, assumptions, and opinions that surround the problem. Assess the accuracy of the information. Then ask "Why?" at least five times to find the root cause of a problem. This technique helps you separate symptoms from underlying problems. Only after completing your diagnosis should you prescribe a solution.

Before you start solving problems, keep this office wall quote in mind: "An appropriate solution to a well-defined problem is much more useful than a great solution to a poorly defined problem."

‘Work Smarter and Harder’

"Work Smarter and Harder"

Change your attitude from "Work smarter, not harder" to "Work smarter *and* harder." Today's competition requires you to do both—working smarter and harder.

Working smarter means eliminating work that your customer doesn't value, and finding the easiest way to complete a task. We all have a certain amount of "busy work" in our daily routine. But how much of it translates into real value for the customer? A good question to ask is: "Is the customer willing to pay for these activities?" Most busy work is obsolete and unnecessary. Eliminate it. The less you do to produce the desired results, the better you will do your job.

A second way to work smarter is to frequently ask the question: "What's the easiest way to complete this task or project?" Certainly, benchmarking and brainstorming are useful tools in discovering easier ways of working. Other things to consider are:

- Could someone else do part or all of the task?
- Could minor changes be made to an existing plan or program?
- Can steps in the work process be eliminated? combined? automated?
- Could the system be changed so you only deal with exceptions?

Since the competition also is striving to work smarter, you sometimes have to work harder and longer to gain the edge. If that's the case, get to work early or stay late. Work Saturday morning or Sunday afternoon. If you have to sacrifice your personal time, then make sure it's time well-spent. Make sure there is value added in all you do—otherwise, your extra effort will be worthless.

Also, know your limits—know when to knock off and take a break. When you finish a project, celebrate!

‘Don’t Ignore the Process’

"Don't Ignore the Process"

Change your focus from "content" (the what) to "process" (the how).

Let's consider what happens at the typical problem-solving meeting. The process involves five steps:

1. Defining the problem
2. Collecting and analyzing data
3. Generating alternatives
4. Evaluating and selecting an alternative
5. Implementing

Because the entire group must work its way through these five steps, it's not uncommon to have people attacking the problem from different points of view. For example, at any given time, one team member may be at Step 1 trying to define the problem, another at Step 3 discussing options, and another at Step 5. In addition, because most problems require multiple meetings, it's easy to see how people can get off track.

Little or no progress is made when everyone on the team is at a different point in the process. When this occurs, you need to bring the group together by asking, "Where are we in the process?" Keep the group focused on resolving one step before moving on to the next. Productivity will improve as the team systematically works through the process.

Also, it's important to do some "consensus taking" as the group works through the process. I usually ask questions to determine the degree of agreement among the group. "Does everyone agree with how we defined the problem?" "Does everyone accept this plan?"

Very often your role is not to have all the answers and solve all the problems. Rather, it's to help the group or team stay focused and follow a structural process.

‘If You Pick It Up, Don’t Put It Down Without Taking Action’

"If You Pick It Up, Don't Put It Down Without Taking Action"

Change from moving paper around your desk from one pile to another to taking action.

Technology promised us the paperless office and then promptly delivered faxes, photocopies, computer printouts, and spreadsheets. Paperwork is everywhere. Kerry Gleeson, head of the Institute of Business Technology, said that white-collar employees deal with each letter or memo an average of five times before acting on it. Moving paper around your desk from one pile to another doesn't make for a productive, efficient operation. The real problem isn't paper—it's decision-making.

If you pick up a piece of paper, do something with it. After reading it, either take action, throw it away, or file it. Taking action could mean writing a response, phoning someone, scheduling a meeting, or asking for additional information. Don't put the paper down without taking action. When I am tempted to postpone a decision about a specific piece of paper, I ask myself, "What am I going to know tomorrow that I don't know today?" Ninety-eight percent of the time you will not know anything more tomorrow, so make a decision, now. Every time I can put something in my out-basket, I get a feeling of accomplishment.

Simply following the "Handle paperwork only once" rule will make you more efficient and productive.

‘Just Do It . . .
Now!’

Change from "procrastinating" to being "action oriented."

Let's face it, we all procrastinate to some degree. Procrastination, however, is in direct opposition to today's emphasis on speed. Process owners must make decisions and take action promptly to satisfy their customers.

If you know what "it" is, then do it. Don't waste a lot of mental energy thinking up reasons why you can't do the task now. Putting aside a job or problem doesn't make it go away. The first step in overcoming procrastination is to identify the thoughts that go through your mind when you find yourself putting things off.

Linda Wachner, CEO of Warnaco, is a firm believer in this motto. She carries a spiral notebook with the words "DO IT NOW" embossed on the cover in big black letters. Mike Walsh, CEO at Tenneco, is also a strong believer in this action-oriented approach. He emphasizes the need for results, not best efforts, and he uses the motto "Just do it" to describe the management intensity at Tenneco.

One of my previous bosses who practices the "Do it now" philosophy had a card on his desk that said:

Do It Now

- Not after lunch
- Not later
- Not tomorrow
- Not next week
- Not when I get around to it
- Now—Do It Now!

Remember, unless there's a very good reason to wait . . .
do it now!

‘Waste Means
Adding Cost
but
Not Adding Value’

"Waste Means Adding Cost but Not Adding Value"

Eliminate waste.

Waste is anything that is unnecessary or doesn't add value. Management consultant Marcus Harwood claims that when he looks at business processes, he tends to find half the activities don't add any real value to the product or service. Customers do not pay for waste. Companies do, by being less competitive. When Jerre Stead became president of Square D Company, he was presented with 4-inch-thick manuals of official corporate policies and procedures—760 rules in all. Many of these policies were bureaucratic, overly complicated, costly, and time-consuming. Mr. Stead dumped the rule book in favor of 11 policy statements. Bravo!

Every business day you face unnecessary meetings, reports, forms, approvals, reviews, rules, regulations, words.

Fighting waste at work is similar to attacking clutter at home. At home we clear out our closets and basement by asking questions such as:

- Do these clothes fit? Are they in style?
- Do I really need four pair of running shoes?
- Have I used this item in the past six months?

In business we need to ask similar questions to clean our work area. Fighting waste and clutter at work is also like fighting weeds in the garden. You have to stay at it and do it on a regular basis.

Your job will be a lot easier and simpler if you eliminate all unnecessary, non-value-adding requirements and activities. Your productivity depends on your ability to simplify, not complicate.

Remember . . . redundant employees are out. Your job is to make sure you're adding value.

‘Quality Achievements Feed on Passion, Commitment, Curiosity, and an Attitude of Continuous Improvement’

"Quality Achievements Feed on Passion, Commitment, Curiosity, and an Attitude of Continuous Improvement"

Change from having a ho-hum attitude toward quality to having a passionate commitment to quality.

The word "quality" has become something of a meaningless buzzword. "Quality is job 1," says an auto ad. Other ads claim quality parts, quality service, quality food. At many of the business meetings and presentations, quality is discussed in a ho-hum fashion. Where's the passion? Real quality is about passion, pride, and commitment to meet and exceed customer requirements.

How can you get excited about quality? You might start by answering these questions:

- Do you really care about your customers?
- Do you really care about helping them satisfy their needs or solve their problem?
- Do you care about their overall satisfaction with your product and service?
- Are you committed to continuously improving all aspects of your operation?

The more you care about your customer, the more motivated you will be to provide "total quality."

Author Richard Pascale takes it a step further. He says that we must move beyond "caring" about quality to "becoming" quality. He believes that just as recruits at basic training become part of the Army, management must acquire a governing philosophy of total quality, to the extent of "becoming" total quality. Only such a profound shift in outlook, he says, will prepare us for the future.

‘Do It Right the First Time’

Change from doing it over to doing it right the first time.

I frequently see this sign posted in companies I visit. It got me wondering, Why do people do it wrong the first time? Lack of training? Poor concentration? The directions are too complicated or incomplete? They don't care?

I try to do things right the first time but don't always succeed. While installing a new garage door opener I read and followed the directions through step 3 but then figured I could proceed on my own. I finished the project only to realize that I had put one part in backwards. The unit had to be disassembled.

One of the reasons the Japanese have good processes is that they try to think of all the possibilities for error *beforehand*, and they set up the process to prevent any improper result. They also make sure people have the training and tools to do it right the first time. My new motto when working at home is to read *all* the instructions, establish a plan, gather the required tools, and begin. Keep in mind that every time something has to be done over, there is a cost of time, effort, and money.

Sometimes your motto needs to be "Correct it quickly." Some processes are just too complicated to do it right the first time. Computer programming is a good example; solving complex math problems is another. What is needed for these processes is a way to check for errors and make corrections quickly. When you do this, lo and behold, the number of mistakes you make goes down, and you begin "doing it right the first time." Getting immediate, constructive feedback and making corrections "in real time" help a person learn complex processes, making them seem easy and eliminating errors in the long run.

‘Benchmark the Best’

"Benchmark the Best"

Change from having an internal focus to an external focus. You may be great within your company, but how do you compare with "world-class" standards?

Ralph Johnson is a first-line supervisor at a small electronics company. Over the past three years his group of 15 associates has reduced the time it takes to assemble and test a PC board from 30 to 22 days. Ralph thought his group was doing a bang-up job—that is, until he read about a competitor who did the same operation in four days. Ralph's reaction: "That can't be. That's impossible." You can't win by comparing yourself with where you were last year.

Organizational psychologist Carla O'Dell, Ph.D., says that without some external example, the goals for improvement are likely to be, "The same as last year plus 5 percent." That won't cut it. External evidence of what other companies are achieving makes stretch goals very real and attainable.

Benchmarking is a process of measuring or comparing your product, service, process, or practice against the best in the world. The process also includes observing and studying the best practices these companies use to achieve outstanding results. How does your product or service stand up against the best in the world? Study how the best companies operate and execute their processes. Beg, borrow, and try out new ideas to improve your operation.

Sam Walton said that he spent more time in his competitors' stores than they did. He readily admits many of his best ideas came from benchmarking—looking for things others are doing *right*! But remember, only imitating or matching the competition won't put you at the head of the pack.

Benchmarking starts by having the right attitude. Carla O'Dell states that you must be humble enough to admit that someone else is better at something and wise enough to learn from them.

‘If You’re Going to Control the Result, You Have to Control the Process’

"If You're Going to Control the Result, You Have to Control the Process"

Change your attention from looking only at the end of the process to looking at all the steps and actions that make up the process.

The way to improve anything is to first understand how it works. A good way to begin is to flowchart your process.

A flowchart is a written description of all the steps, actions, and decisions required to complete a work process, such as manufacturing a product or purchasing a part. Flowcharting helps you understand what's really going on in a process from start to finish. Flowcharts often reveal how inefficient an operation or process has become. The first flowchart the Titeflex Company made of a process showed that a part traveled 3.5 miles through 14 departments. Do you think their process could be simplified?

At Hamilton Standard, I was on a team that flowcharted the process used to promote or transfer people to other jobs or departments. We found eight steps in the process; four were redundant and were eliminated.

Once you have your process flowcharted, you need to ask questions like the following:

- Could the entire process be eliminated?
- Are all steps needed? Could some steps be combined?
- What are the accuracy and reliability of the information as it passes from step to step?
- What controls, if any, are needed at each step in the process?
- If we were starting with a clean piece of paper, how would the process be designed?

Answers to questions like these help you eliminate waste and improve the process you manage or operate.

‘If My End of the Boat Sinks— So Does Yours’

"If My End of the Boat Sinks—So Does Yours"

Don't just think about yourself, think about your team.

Chances are you're part of a team—probably many teams, whether formal or informal. Effective teams work together to help keep the boat afloat and headed in the right direction. They develop a common purpose, share the leadership role, and hold one another accountable for achieving desired results. To be an effective team member, you need to do the following:

- Put team goals, problems, and initiatives ahead of your own.
- Openly share your ideas and fully consider other points of view.
- Support and encourage team members.
- Complete action items on time and hold others accountable for completion of their action items.

The essence of a team is common commitment. Without it, groups perform as individuals. The challenge is to find the right balance of being a team player without being a "yes person." There are times when you must show leadership and challenge team members. Disagreements and conflicts are healthy and productive when conducted in a professional manner.

However, a major detractor to effective teamwork is *ongoing* and *unresolved* conflicts. Note the emphasis on "ongoing" and "unresolved." These types of conflicts are unhealthy and tend to split teams into factions. In this situation, team members spend more time and energy focusing on the conflict than on the task at hand. What's the solution? Teams need to call a time-out and deal with the unresolved issues.

Remember, a team saddled with unresolved conflicts cannot compete with a team that is focused and aligned.

‘Not Everything That Counts Can Be Counted’

Change from focusing only on what you can count or measure to focusing on the things you can't measure, such as vision and values. Certainly, hard numbers like cost, profit, and cycle time are important, but soft things like vision and values are the building blocks of everything you do.

A vision is a mental picture of a desired future. A mental picture helps you see yourself not as you are but as you can become.

What's your vision for yourself? your team? If you don't have a vision, a good place to start is to think about what gets you excited. What cause or dream gets your adrenaline pumping?

Other points to keep in mind when developing your vision:

- Aim high. You and your team will not work hard and make sacrifices to achieve insignificant results. Another office wall quote stated: "Great vision precedes great accomplishment."
- Keep it simple. An overly complex vision doesn't act as an inspirational guide, but rather causes confusion and acts as a turn-off. Boil your vision down to one or two sentences.
- Discuss it. Discuss your vision with friends and associates. Doing this not only helps you clarify your vision but also helps you learn how to communicate it clearly and succinctly.

Values, beliefs, and principles are also very important. They make up the foundation on which you and your team operate. Effective teams establish operating principles and team members hold one another accountable to that standard. When values and principles are violated, people and teams start to fall apart.

The bottom-line message—pay attention to the things you can't count. They are the foundation upon which everything else is built.

‘Leadership
Is Lifting
People’s Vision,
Values,
and Confidence
to a New Level’

Change from "push" to "pull."

One way to influence people is to push them into action—ordering them or directing them to do such and such. Traditional supervisors and managers have performed this role. Under this scenario, employees wait to be told what to do, how to do it, etc. Their initiative, their willingness to take risks and make decisions to satisfy customers, dissipates.

In today's business environment, people need to be "pulled" along. Pull techniques involve creating an environment in which people do things not because they have to but because they want to. They feel and act like owners. Leaders who "pull people" along allow for a great deal of discussion and participation about topics such as values, beliefs, and visions of the future. What emerges out of these discussions is a vision and a set of principles so clear and so compelling that people are willing to work 10- and 12-hour days to achieve this desired future state.

At various times, all employees are required to take a leadership role. Leaders provide people with what they can't do for themselves. At various times people need courage, confidence, coaching, a vision of what's possible, and guidance in how to achieve desired results. Effective leaders serve others and provide what's needed to help people grow, develop and succeed.

When it's your turn to lead, figure out what the person or group needs and then take action. Keep in mind this advice from management guru Peter Drucker. He says that leadership is about lifting a person's vision to higher sights, raising a person's performance to a new standard, and building a personality to reach its full potential.

‘You Can’t Steal Second Base and Keep One Foot on First’

"You Can't Steal Second Base and Keep One Foot on First"

Change from waffling to deciding!

My children get upset when they ask permission to do something and I respond with that parental phrase "We'll see" or "I'll think about it." They prefer an instant response of "Yes" or "No" to an excessively long-drawn-out "Maybe." President Harry S. Truman used to quip that he was looking for a one-armed economist, one who could never say, "On the one hand this, but on the other hand that."

Making decisions and taking risks are a requirement of all employees. To satisfy customers, quickly and effectively, process owners must make decisions about cost, schedule, and quality. Be decisive. Waffling won't cut it in today's fast-paced environment.

When I start waffling on a decision, I think back to when I coached hockey. During a game I had to make immediate decisions. In the middle of a game you can't say, "I'm going to form a committee to study this problem" or "I'll get back to you tomorrow." No, you must decide on the spot. These coaching flashbacks remind me to make a decision and move on.

A senior executive at a New York bank says, "We make it clear to new employees that there will always be uncertain or unknowable factors in a situation. We want them to collect and consider all relevant information. But overstudy can't be a substitute for decision-making."

Don't waste your time searching for that last 5 percent of critical information—it doesn't exist. Make a decision: Either steal second or stay on first.

‘Walk the Talk’

Change from "talking" to "modeling."

In this book, I've advocated many changes you must make to grow and prosper in your career. If I only talk about these changes and don't practice what I preach, my credibility is lost. It reminds me of my high school coach. At the beginning of the season he said, "Men, during the season I *don't* want you to smoke or drink, and I *do* want you to run and lift weights to stay in shape." As we watched our coach, he drank, smoked, and never ran, lifted weights, or did anything to stay physically fit.

This coach had very little credibility and in turn had little impact on the team and myself. As Ralph Waldo Emerson stated, "What you do is so loud, I can't hear what you say."

To have credibility you must model the values, principles, and beliefs that you espouse. As a positive role model you demonstrate or show what good performance looks like. If people can see the desired performance, they are more likely to hit the mark. If you preach "customer focus," "teamwork" and "taking risks, make sure your behavior matches your words.

I know a vice president of engineering who constantly preaches lifelong learning. In staff meetings and speeches he urges people to continue their education by attending seminars and taking college courses. At age 63, he continues to practice what he preaches. Every semester he enrolls in college classes—philosophy, history, psychology, software engineering, etc. He also attends two to three seminars per year. He "walks the talk" and as a result has great credibility.

‘Everything Looks Like a Failure in the Middle’

Change from "giving up" to "pressing on."

Change is hard work. During a major change, there are usually two or three critical points when I have a mental battle with myself. Negative thoughts and doubts begin to creep in. "This won't work; it's not worth the effort." Depending on how I handle these critical moments the change effort is won or lost. Many people give up at just the time when if they hung in there a little longer, they would have achieved success. There's a lot to be said for determination and persistence.

When Herschel Walker was in junior high school his coach told him: "Herschel, you're too small for football. You should try track." Walker's response was to undertake an exercise and running program to build himself into an All-American football player and Heisman Trophy winner. He said that his God-given talent was his ability to stick with it longer than anyone else.

Don't get discouraged if your ideas aren't enthusiastically supported right away. It's easy to quit, but that doesn't solve anything. If you believe in your idea, work on building support slowly. President Calvin Coolidge said, "The slogan 'Press on' has solved and always will solve the problems of the human race."

Remember that the steady drip-drip-drip of persistence produces results and long-term success.

‘Failure Is
Not an End,
if It’s Viewed
as a
Learning Experience’

"Failure Is Not an End, if It's Viewed as a Learning Experience"

Change your view of failure.

What is failure? Flunking a course? Blowing a presentation? Losing a key customer? Getting fired from a job? Failure has more to do with attitude than specific circumstances. As long as you keep learning, experimenting, and working to achieve your goals you haven't failed. Failure occurs only when you stop trying, when you give up, when you quit.

Abraham Lincoln lost eight straight elections before he finally won the big one. He wasn't afraid of failure. Some people cushion themselves against failure by never really trying. If you never take risks and challenge your "comfort zone," you'll never know what you can achieve. The biggest challenge is not out there in the marketplace but is the journey you find in yourself. When you take risks and face difficult challenges, the biggest prize is the courage, self-knowledge, and self-confidence you attain. Self-confidence is the ability to face fear and failure with emotional stability and determination.

When failure occurs, it needs to be a growth experience. Some people never learn how to react to failure. They become defensive and consequently never learn or grow from the experience. They will make the same mistake in the future. If you listen calmly and keep an open mind, you will grow from the experience. Critique your failures. Those lessons learned the hard way usually provide the building blocks to future successes. Make using "lessons learned" a daily part of how to work smarter—faster—better.

‘Be Kind.
Everyone You Meet
Is Fighting
a Tough Battle’

"Be Kind. Everyone You Meet Is Fighting a Tough Battle"

Change from "lean and mean" to "lean and nice."

In today's competitive business environment with all the budget cuts and downsizing, just about everyone is overworked and overstressed. Even customers are fighting tough battles.

A key characteristic of good leadership is the ability to show empathy. Put yourself in the other person's shoes. Be kind, patient, and understanding with people and they will often repay you in a like manner. The Golden Rule still applies in all areas of life.

Every Saturday my family and I go out for breakfast. We drive about five miles to a small restaurant. On the way we pass four other restaurants. We have tried each of these but chose not to return. We keep returning to our favorite spot because the waitress is superb. Even though she's overworked, she's friendly, caring, and kind. The food isn't better at this restaurant, but the overall experience is considerably better because of her gentle, considerate nature.

If you are "kind," you may even get more than kindness in return. A few years ago a national newspaper carried a story about a waitress who for many years served an old man dressed in tattered clothing. Every day when he came into the coffee shop, she was kind to him and always found time to chat and listen. One day the man died . . . and several months later she found out he had bequeathed her $200,000 in his will!

The previous sections have shown why a positive attitude can carry you far. Where does a positive attitude come from? Try being kind and focus on other people, not yourself, and observe the positive impact on your attitude.

‘I Love This Place’

Change from "My job's OK, I guess" to "I love my job!"

Don't stick around just to collect the gold watch. Stick around because your work is exciting, challenging, and rewarding. A senior manager at RJR Nabisco described his passion for work when he made this comment: "One Sunday night I turned to my wife and said, 'I really can't wait to get to the office tomorrow.' "

My wife, Mary Jean is passionate about her job. Her day often starts with a 7:30 a.m. meeting and often ends at 10:00 p.m. sending voice-mail messages. She told me that although work is demanding and stressful, it's also exciting and satisfying. She said, "Watching people excel after you have given them responsibility and authority and helped them grow and develop makes it all worthwhile." She tells our children, "Find out what you value, what's really important to you and passion will follow."

Do you love your work? Have you found joy and excitement in your job? If you really don't like your job, figure out why and then start the journey to find out what type of work makes you excited, passionate, and creative. Develop a plan to achieve your new career goal. Or perhaps you can redesign your current job to maximize the assignments you find challenging and rewarding.

Think what might happen if you fell in love with your work. Wouldn't it be great!

Find a job to love!

How many hours till Monday?

To summarize . . .

These office wall quotes provide valuable insight and advice about what's needed to succeed and prosper in your business and career. The real message—change. Changing times call for changing attitudes, behaviors, plans, and partnerships. Here's what you need to do:

Deliver products and services faster, with lower cost and greater quality. And it goes without saying that your products and services must satisfy the customers and get them to say "Wow!" or "Gee whiz, look at this" once in a while.

Anticipate and respond appropriately to changing customer needs, new ways of working, and a dynamic marketplace. Be flexible and open to new ideas. Risk-taking is a must.

Continually improve your knowledge, skills, attitude, motivation, and commitment to excellence. Lifelong learning and improvement are essential in today's competitive marketplace. Do your homework, plan ahead, and don't quit.

Finally, benchmark. Compare your processes and products with the best in the world.

And remember, when you visit business associates, customers, suppliers, and competitors, check out what's posted in their work areas. These nuggets of gold may give you additional ideas about how to achieve your business and career goals.

What's posted in your office area?

I'd be pleased to hear from you regarding *The Answers Are on the Office Wall*. Also please send me any quotes you have posted in your work area. You may write to me at: 90 Fairway Drive, Chicopee, MA 01020. Thank you.

References and Bibliography

Articles

Case, J. "A Company of Business People," *Inc.*, April 1993, pp. 79-93.

Gissing, B. "Quality as a Competitive Strategy: A Rediscovery." Speech delivered at the Planning Forum Management Conference, Toronto, Canada, April 29, 1991.

Kirkpatrick, D. "Could AT&T Rule the World?" *Fortune*, May 1993, pp. 54-66.

Sellers, P., and Kirkpatrick, D. "Can This Man Save IBM?"*Fortune*, April 1993, pp. 63-67.

Thornton, P. B. "Teamwork: Focus, Frame, Facilitate," *Management Review*, November 1992, pp. 46-47.

Tichy, N., and Charan, R. "Speed, Simplicity, Self-Confidence: An Interview with Jack Welch," *Harvard Business Review*, September/October 1989, pp. 112-120.

Webber, A. M. "What's So New About the New Economy?" *Harvard Business Review*, January/February 1993, pp. 24-42.

Weston, J. S. "Soft Stuff Matters," *Personal Selling Power*, May/June 1993, pp. 50-55.

Books

Covey, S. R. *The 7 Habits of Highly Effective People*. New York: Simon & Schuster, 1990.

Drucker, P. F. *The Effective Executive*. New York: Harper & Row, 1966.

Elgin, S. H. *Success With the Gentle Art of Verbal Self-Defense*. Englewood Cliffs, NJ: Prentice-Hall, 1989.

Fromm, W. *The Ten Commandments of Business and How to Break Them*. New York: G. P. Putnam's Sons, 1991.
Garfield, C. *Peak Performers*. New York: Avon Books, 1986.
Kriegel, R. J. *If It Ain't Broke . . . Break It*. New York: Warner Books, 1991.
Mackay, H. *Swim With the Sharks Without Being Eaten Alive*. New York: William Morrow and Co., 1988.
Peters, T., and Austin, N. *A Passion for Excellence*. New York: Random House, 1985.
Pritchett, P. *Culture Shift*. Dallas, TX: Pritchett Publishing, 1993.
Senge, P. M. *The Fifth Discipline*. New York: Doubleday, 1990.
Smith, M. R. *Contrarian Management*. New York: American Management Association, 1992.
Thornton, P. B. *Lessons from the Best Managers*. Morrisville, PA: International Information Associates, 1991.
Whiteley, R. C. *The Customer-Driven Company*. Reading, MA: Addison-Wesley, 1991.
Willingham, R. *Hey, I'm the Customer*. Englewood Cliffs, NJ: Prentice Hall, 1992.